source to resource

FROM
OIL RIG
TO
GAS PUMP

MICHAEL BRIGHT

Crabtree Publishing Company
www.crabtreebooks.com

Crabtree Publishing Company
www.crabtreebooks.com
1-800-387-7650

Published in Canada
Crabtree Publishing
616 Welland Avenue
St. Catharines, ON
L2M 5V6

Published in the United States
Crabtree Publishing
PMB 59051
350 Fifth Ave, 59th Floor
New York, NY 10118

Author: Michael Bright

Editorial director: Kathy Middleton

Freelance editor: Katie Woolley

Editors: Annabel Stones, Liza Miller, and Ellen Rodger

Designer: Rocket Design Ltd

Proofreader: Wendy Scavuzzo

Prepress technician: Samara Parent

Print and production coordinator: Katherine Berti

Published by Crabtree Publishing Company in 2017

First published in 2016 by Wayland
(A division of Hachette Children's Books)
Copyright © Wayland, 2016

Printed in Canada/072016/PB20160525

Photographs:
Cover: Terry Williams/Getty; p 7 (top): Lloyd Cluff/Corbis, p 8: Imagestate Media Partners Limited – Impact Photos/Alamy Stock Photo, p 9 (left): Corbis; p 9 (right): GL Archive/Alamy Stock Photo, p 12: Joel Sartore/National Geographic Creative/Corbis; p 25: Natalie Fobes/Science Faction/Corbis.

All other images and graphic elements courtesy of Shutterstock

Illustrations:
Stefan Chabluk: p 10; p19; p 30

Library and Archives Canada Cataloguing in Publication

Bright, Michael, author
    From oil rig to gas pump / Michael Bright.

(Source to resource)
Includes index.
Issued in print and electronic formats.
ISBN 978-0-7787-2706-4 (hardback).--
ISBN 978-0-7787-2710-1 (paperback).--
ISBN 978-1-4271-1816-5 (html)

    1. Petroleum industry and trade--Juvenile literature.
2. Petroleum industry and trade--Environmental aspects--Juvenile literature. I. Title.

HD9560.5.B695 2016   j333.8'232   C2016-902591-8
                                                 C2016-902592-6

Library of Congress Cataloging-in-Publication Data

CIP available at the Library of Congress

Contents

Oil

Oil is one of the most important products of the modern age. Vehicles depend on it for fuel, and it is essential for the manufacturing of many goods. If oil supplies suddenly ran out, modern life would grind to a halt—at least for now.

Petroleum

The word **petroleum** is Latin for "rock oil," which means oil found inside rocks. Petroleum is the main source of gas and diesel fuel for cars and trucks. It is also used in the generation of electricity in power stations, and in the manufacturing of products such as plastics and car tires. Petroleum is the resource we will follow from oil rig to gas pump.

Renewable and non-renewable

Petroleum is a **non-renewable** energy source. The sun, wind, and ocean waves are renewable energy sources because they will never run out. Petroleum can only be used once, and one day it will all be used up.

Large quantities of petroleum are extracted from rocks underneath the seabed.

Oil from the olive tree is mostly used for cooking, but it can also be used as biofuel for cars.

Nodding donkeys

One of the most iconic images of the oil industry is said to look like a nodding donkey. It is a pump that pulls oil from a well. It was a common sight in the oil booms of the early 1900s, and large numbers of these pumps can still be seen today, silently nodding away in oil-rich areas.

Animal and plant oils

Animals and plants also provide different types of oil. Cod liver oil is made from cod fish, and people take it to boost their intake of vitamins. Plant or vegetable oils are made from nuts, seeds, and fruits, and include olive oil, sunflower oil, and coconut oil. These oils are mainly used for cooking, but some plant oils can be turned into biofuel and used to power cars and trucks.

Oil origins

Petroleum is made from the fossilized remains of creatures that lived up to 180 million years ago. Most were plankton **from ancient seas and lakes, but larger animals, such as dinosaurs, probably formed part of the remains as well. For this reason, petroleum is known as a** fossil fuel.

Ancient plankton is the basic ingredient of oil.

Oil formation

Petroleum formed when the dead bodies of living things fell to the seabed. Over time, layer upon layer of sand and mud covered them. Then, over millions of years, high temperatures and intense pressure "cooked" the remains. This formed the liquid petroleum and **natural gas** that is now hidden within rocks deep underground.

Oil seeps

Most petroleum is locked away deep beneath the earth, but sometimes cracks in the rocks allow some oil to escape to the surface. These are known as oil or petroleum seeps. They can occur on land or beneath the sea, and often produce **bitumen**, which is also known as asphalt or tar. Tar has been used by people for centuries, for many different purposes.

Asphalt lakes are a mix of asphalt, natural gas, water, sand, and clay.

Animal trap

A tar pit or asphalt lake is a petroleum seep where asphalt forms a thick, black, sticky lake on the surface of Earth. The most famous are the La Brea Tar Pits in Los Angeles. There, the bones of prehistoric animals, such as saber-toothed cats, dire wolves, and mastodons, have been preserved. The animals probably fell accidentally into the asphalt, became trapped, and then died there.

Asphalt volcanoes

An asphalt volcano was first discovered in 2003, on the floor of the Gulf of Mexico. Asphalt volcanoes are undersea mountains that form over oil seeps oozing from the seabed. They erupt bitumen, natural gas, and liquid petroleum instead of lava. Asphalt volcanoes and their resources have yet to be explored.

DID YOU KNOW?

Trinidad's Pitch Lake is the largest asphalt lake in the world. It covers an area the size of nearly 50 football fields and is 249 ft (76 m) deep in the center.

History of oil

We think of petroleum as a modern resource, but people have used it in one form or another for thousands of years. At first, bitumen from seeps was collected from the surface. Then, at least 2,000 years ago, the first oil and gas wells were drilled in Asia.

Ancient asphalt roads

The earliest known use of bitumen was by the Neanderthals 40,000 years ago. They used it to glue stone ax heads to wooden shafts. In 615 B.C.E., it was used in ancient Mesopotamia to surface the road from King Nabopolassar's palace to the north wall of the city of Babylon. Sometime later, the ancient Romans used bitumen to seal public baths, **reservoirs**, and **aqueducts**.

The ancient brick and asphalt Procession Road in Babylon can still be seen today.

First oil and gas drilling

About 2,000 years ago, the Chinese drilled for underground **brine** lakes using drill bits on the end of sturdy bamboo poles. While doing this, they discovered oil and gas. The Chinese burned the oil and gas and used the heat to boil away the water in the brine, leaving behind salt crystals which they used for cooking.

Oil rush

In Pennsylvania, in 1859, Edwin Drake erected what is thought to be the world's first modern oil well. This started a major oil boom, known as the Pennsylvania Oil Rush, which continued until the 1870s. Oil was first used for lighting homes, replacing whale oil. After Henry Ford invented the affordable **mass-produced** Model T Ford car in 1908, oil became even more important—for transportation.

Early oil wells frequently had **blowouts**. It was very dangerous if the oil and gas caught fire.

Henry Ford invented the first mass-produced car.

Did You Know?

In about 672 C.E., the Byzantine navy often used a weapon known as "Greek Fire." The sailors squirted a mixture of flammable chemicals, including oil, on the sea's surface and over enemy ships — then set it on fire. They won many sea battles that way.

9

Searching for oil

Petroleum is found all over the world, but to pinpoint the best places to drill, geologists search for certain telltale signs that show where it might have pooled in large quantities. They can look for seeps at the surface, but most oil exploration today is done with special equipment that explores deep underground.

The right rocks

Geologists first look for areas with the right types of rock. Petroleum is often found in **porous** sandstone and limestone. There is usually a cap of hard rock on top of the oil reservoir that stops it from escaping to the surface.

Explosive exploration

If an area seems promising, a more detailed investigation is done. One way is to use air guns or explosives to fire sounds down into the ground. Echoes then bounce off the different rock layers and are recorded. From this, a three-dimensional map of the area can be created.

BRAINY BITS

A reservoir of natural gas sometimes sits on top of the oil layer.

Oil is often found where rocks are formed into a dome shape.

The oil well taps into the oil layer.

Exploratory drilling

Drilling is the only sure way of discovering if there is oil. Onshore, or on land, a drilling **derrick** is built. This is a frame built over the oil well that can lift heavy loads of oil from the ground. As the drilling machinery digs into the ground, artificial mud is pumped into the hole. This cools the drill bit and flushes out broken pieces of rock, which geologists can analyze. If the drill reaches an oil reservoir, the oil will sometimes squirt out like a huge fountain, known to oil workers as a gusher.

Drilling at sea

At sea, drilling is more difficult. The offshore rig must be stable enough to withstand winds, waves, and tides or the drill shaft will break. There are three types of rigs, depending on the depth of water. In shallow water, a barge converts to a platform with legs that reach the seabed. In slightly deeper water, the platform has submerged floats that keep the rig steady, so rough seas are less noticeable. In deep water, giant anchors or computer-controlled propellers keep the drilling rig in place.

An onshore drilling rig.

Floats or pontoons below the surface keep this offshore drilling rig afloat.

Extracting oil

When geologists have confirmed that petroleum is where they thought it was, the area becomes known as an oil field. It is then the task of engineers to bring it up to the surface and transport it away.

Oil wells

On land, the **wellhead** is capped with a pump and a complicated stack of **valves** known as the "Christmas tree." Extraction is done in two phases. During phase one, some oil comes out of the ground under natural pressure. During phase two, steam, gas, or water is pumped down a connecting well to flush out more oil.

Dangerous blowouts!

A major problem for oil wells is the failure of safety valves, resulting in an uncontrolled blowout. It happened frequently in the early days of oil extraction, but today's equipment is more reliable, so blowouts are less common.

A blowout must be brought under control before it bursts into flames.

Offshore oil platforms

At sea, the pumping must be carried out on a production platform high above the waves. First, ready-built sections of the platform are brought in. Huge cranes then lower the supports onto the seabed and the platform is placed securely on top. It must reach above the largest waves, which can be hundreds of feet high!

Floating cities

The platforms can be huge, and several platforms can be joined together by footbridges. They are like tiny towns, with bedrooms, cafeterias, movie theaters, gyms, offices, and stores. There is usually also a helipad to transport workers to and from the mainland by helicopter.

A "Christmas tree" with several valves caps the top of the oil well.

Deep-sea submarines

Maintenance of the supports and wellheads of offshore oil platforms is carried out in deep water, so manned and unmanned **submersibles** are often sent down. Crews will sometimes spot mysterious deep-sea creatures swimming around them.

Crude oil

The raw petroleum that comes out of the ground is known as crude oil. Oil prospectors call it "black gold." There are many different types of crude oil, each one with a different consistency, color, and chemical makeup. It can be yellow and runny like water, or black and thick like sludge.

Light and heavy

A key difference between the different types of crude oil is weight. Lighter crude oil is more valuable than heavier crude. The light crude is easily converted into valuable products, such as gasoline. Heavy crude requires more expensive processing to produce the same fuels.

Some crude oil is very black, earning the name "black gold."

These steel barrels are holding large quantities of crude oil.

Sweet and sour

A second difference is sulfur content. If the crude oil is low in chemical sulfur, it is described as "sweet." If it is high in sulfur, it is called "sour." Sulfur damages metal pipes and is costly to remove, so oil workers prefer to have crude oil with a low sulfur content.

Life in crude

Tiny living things called **bacteria** are known to live in oil. More surprisingly, a type of insect does too! When oil seeps onto land, it attracts petroleum flies. Their **larvae** feed on the dead insects trapped in the petroleum pools. They are the only animals known to live in crude oil.

Barrels of oil

Oil is sometimes shipped in 55-gallon (208 L) barrels. Oil markets in the United States and Canada tend to use a barrel based on the Old English wine barrel known as a tierce, which can hold 42 gallons (159 L).

DID YOU KNOW?

Half of all crude oil that enters coastal waters comes not from accidental oil spills, but from natural petroleum seeps on the seabed.

15

Transporting crude oil

Crude oil is carried from oil field to oil refinery either by pipe or by ship. Pipelines are preferred because they are the cheapest way to move oil. If all the oil pipelines in the United States were laid end to end, they would almost reach the moon!

Pipelines

Oil pipelines are made either with plastic or steel. On land they are generally hidden underground, but in the Arctic they are carried on stilts above the frozen **tundra**.

Pipelines also lie on the seabed, carrying crude oil from offshore oil fields to mainland oil refineries. Separate pipelines take refined oil products from refineries to distribution centers.

The 795-mile (1,280 km) Trans-Alaska Pipeline carries oil across the tundra. The pipes are 48 inches (122 cm) in diameter.

Oil supertankers are huge. When going full speed, they can take 5.5 miles (9 km) to come to a complete stop!

Supertankers

Oil supertankers are among the world's largest ships. Some are as long as the Empire State Building is tall! They can carry up to three million barrels of oil at a time. When fully loaded, they can only travel at 16 knots, or 18 mph (29 kph). Like the pipelines, there are giant crude tankers for crude oil, and separate smaller tankers for refined gasoline and other oil products.

Floating storage

Some older oil tankers no longer transport oil around the world. Instead, they are now floating storage and offloading vessels. They are moored to the seabed, close to offshore oil platforms, where they store the crude oil until other tankers arrive to transport it away.

Old oil tankers store crude oil at the drilling site.

DID YOU KNOW?

The world's longest oil pipeline is the Druzhba Pipeline, also known as the Friendship Pipeline. It runs for about 2,485 miles (4,000 km) from the oil city of Almetyevsk, in the Russian Republic of Tatarstan, to Ukraine, Belarus, Poland, Hungary, Slovakia, the Czech Republic, and Germany.

Oil refineries

Crude oil generally needs to be processed before it can be sent to the gas pump as fuel for cars and trucks. The exception is very light crude oil with a low sulfur content, which can be used directly as fuel for large ships.

The refinery

Crude oil is processed in an oil refinery. Many different processes are carried out to break down crude oil and recover useful fuels and other products. Many refineries operate continually, processing hundreds of thousands of barrels of crude oil a day.

Boiling oil

One of the main processes in an oil refinery is to separate crude oil into its different products. Crude oil is heated in a furnace and its various parts will evaporate at different temperatures. Gasoline boils off at 320 °F (160 °C), while diesel boils off at 572 °F (300 °C). The vapors or gases from the boiling process collect in a tall, slender tower. There, they cool and become liquid again, but the liquid gasoline and diesel collect in separate trays at different heights in the tower. The lighter gas gathers near the top of the tower and the heavier diesel fuel is found farther down. The liquids are then carried away in separate pipes and stored in tanks.

Oil refineries are a complicated maze of pipes, tanks, and towers.

Oil distillation process

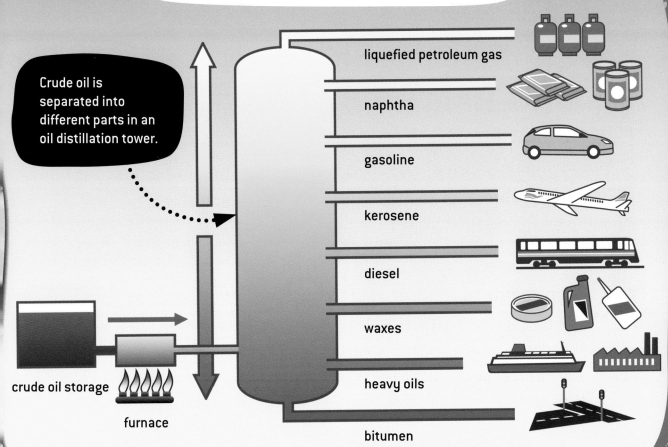

Crude oil is separated into different parts in an oil distillation tower.

- liquefied petroleum gas
- naphtha
- gasoline
- kerosene
- diesel
- waxes
- heavy oils
- bitumen

crude oil storage

furnace

Clean up and modify

Before they can be used, the various oil products need to be cleaned of any dirt or impurities, and some go through more processing. Gasoline, for example, may be modified with **additives** so that a car's engine works more efficiently. Colors are also added to identify types of fuel, such as diesel fuel dyed red for use in farm or construction equipment.

Giant oil complex

The world's largest oil refinery complex is the Jamnagar Refinery in northwest India. There are several refineries on the site, and altogether they can process 1.24 million barrels of oil per day. Together with port facilities, housing for workers, and factories for various manufacturing industries, the entire site is as large as many cities.

Crude oil products

Several different kinds of fuels and other materials can be obtained directly from crude oil. They each have a different chemical makeup and are used in different types of engines or heating systems, or to make petroleum-based products. One is a gas, others are liquid, and some are almost solid.

Gas for camp stoves comes from crude oil.

A cargo plane is refueled.

☀ Liquefied petroleum gas

The kind of gas used in camping stoves and as bottled gas for heaters.

☀ Naphtha

A liquid chemical used in the making of plastics, medicines, and other products (see pages 26–27).

☀ Gasoline

The liquid bought at the gas pump as fuel for cars, some trucks, and small boats.

☀ Kerosene

A liquid used as fuel for jet aircraft. In the home, it can be used as heating oil in paraffin heaters and in kerosene lamps. In Asia, kerosene is used as fuel for some small fishing boats.

☀ Diesel

Diesel is thicker than kerosene and is used as a fuel for diesel-powered cars, vans, trucks, trains, and ships.

 Waxes

Most candles used in the home are made from petroleum-based wax. Wax is also used to waterproof food cartons, such as milk containers

Heavy oils

These include oils to keep engines running smoothly, as well as fuels for ships, factory boilers, and electricity-generating power stations.

 Bitumen

This dark, thick, and sometimes solid material becomes soft and sticky when it is heated. Also known as asphalt or tar, it is used on road surfaces and in roofing materials.

Bitumen is a commonly used road surface.

Riches in a barrel

One 42-gallon (159 L) barrel of crude oil makes approximately:

GASOLINE 20 gallons (76 L)

DIESEL 10 gallons (38 L)

BITUMEN 6.6 gallons (25 L)

KEROSENE FOR JET FUEL 4 gallons (15 L)

KEROSENE FOR HEATING OIL 2 gallons (8 L)

Fuel to the pump

Gas and diesel fuel for cars and trucks is delivered by pipelines, ships, and trains to storage tanks at distribution centers. From there, trucks load up and deliver the fuel to individual gas stations.

Fuel tanker trucks are designed not to spill their load if they crash or overturn.

Road tankers

Fuel tankers typically have a cylindrical tank that lies horizontally on the truck or on a trailer. Pipes, valves, and safety systems on the tanker ensure that the transfer of fuel is safe, from the distribution center to the tanker, and from the tanker to the gas station.

Gas station

Underneath the station's fuel pumps there are several separate storage tanks. Each tank contains a different type of gasoline or diesel fuel. When a customer selects the type of fuel they need, the correct fuel feeds from the tank to the pump.

Gas pump

There are several types of gas pumps and delivery systems. The most common is a pump linked electronically to a central control panel behind the counter in the gas station. Customers serve themselves, then pay at the counter. Many stations also have a credit card reader attached to the pump, so customers can pay right at the pump, 24 hours a day.

Gasoline can ignite easily. It is extremely dangerous to smoke cigarettes or light matches near a car that is being fueled at a gas station.

Automatic cut-off

When a car's fuel tank is almost full, an automatic cut-off valve stops the flow of gas. Inside the mouth of the nozzle there is a sensing tube that leads to a valve in the pump handle. A change of **air pressure** is detected as the tank fills up, causing the valve to shut.

A gas pump nozzle has two pipes inside.

Unleaded and leaded

Most gas stations sell diesel fuel and a few types of unleaded gas. At one time, all gas-fueled cars ran on leaded gas, which had a chemical containing lead added to it to make cars work better. Unfortunately, lead was also in the waste gases that came out of the car's exhaust pipe. It **polluted** the air, especially in cities, and turned out to be very dangerous for people's health. Most countries have now banned leaded gas.

23

Oil incidents

At every stage, from oil exploration to the gas pump, petroleum and many of its products can be dangerous to people and the environment. Oil and transportation companies try to minimize the risks but accidents do happen, and when they do, they are often devastating.

Oil rig blowouts

If something goes wrong at the wellhead, enormous quantities of oil and natural gas can burst out. This can easily catch fire and cause damaging explosions and intense heat. These fires are difficult to put out because so much fuel is involved. They are sometimes extinguished using dynamite. The explosion blows away the fuel and oxygen, starving the fire, like blowing out a candle.

On the rocks

If an oil tanker hits rocks and its hull is damaged, large quantities of crude oil can spill into the ocean. Wildlife often suffers the most. The feathers of seabirds become coated with oil, and a black sheen of oil smothers the seashore and anything living there.

An oil well fire will burn as long as there is oil, gas, and oxygen to feed it.

When oil spills happen, birds and other wildlife suffer.

Refinery firestorms

The most dangerous time in an oil refinery is during its maintenance periods. Operations have to be shut down, and equipment, tools, and pipes are checked thoroughly. Up to 30,000 different procedures have to be carried out, often involving dangerous chemicals. If anything goes wrong, flammable gases can catch fire and cause an enormous explosion.

Deepwater Horizon

The world's worst oil disaster was in the Gulf of Mexico in April 2010. The oil-drilling rig Deepwater Horizon exploded, killing 11 crewmen. The uncapped oil well, gushing on the seabed, caused the largest accidental oil spill ever in the sea. It had a devastating and long-lasting effect on marine life, as well as the fishing industry.

Crude oil is lighter than water. This is why it floats on the surface of the sea.

DID YOU KNOW?

Jet aircraft engines have been used to spray water at the base of oil well fires to put them out. This method was used in 1990 to deal with oil well fires after the Iraq-Kuwait war.

Petroleum-based products

Other than fuel, petroleum is also used to make many products for the home and office. The companies that make them, along with the oil companies, are all part of the petrochemical industry.

✸ Medicines

Petroleum has been used in medicines for centuries. It was once used to try to treat frostbite. Today, oil products are a vital part of medicine. The chemical acetylsalicylic acid, or ASA, is made from oil. It is the active ingredient in painkillers, more commonly known as aspirin.

Painkillers, antibiotics, and cough syrups are all made from oil. The plastic bottles they come in are also made from oil.

✸ Comfortable clothes

Oil is used to make **synthetic** fibers and fabrics, such as polyester, acrylic, and nylon. They are made into clothes or woven into curtains and carpets. Artificial fur and wigs are also made from these fibers.

✸ Comfortable ride

Car tires are made from a mixture of natural and synthetic rubber. Synthetic rubber is made from oil. Similarly, the soles of shoes can be made from a mixture of different types of rubber.

✸ Sweet tooth

Glycerin is a sweet-tasting ingredient in toothpaste and sugary treats. It is also made from oil.

Personal care products from baby oils to body lotions are made from oil.

❋ Mineral oil

This clear liquid is used in baby oil and cosmetics, among other things.

❋ Growing and protecting plants

Some of the chemicals in fertilizers that increase crop yields come from oil. Oil-based chemicals are also found in pesticides, which protect crops from pests.

❋ Washing up

Detergents are cleaning products made without soap. They are used in dishwashers and washing machines and contain petrochemical products.

❋ Cosmetics

Make-up, nail polish, lipstick, and hair dyes are partly made from oil products.

❋ Packaging

Styrofoam is an oil product used in most of the protective packaging for products. It is also used in food product containers, plastic bottles, and plastic cutlery.

Oil: the future

Modern civilization currently depends on oil, but it is a non-renewable resource. The world's supply of oil will one day run out. In the quest for cleaner, more reliable sources of energy, fuel oil is slowly being replaced by renewable resources, such as solar and wind power. So, does oil have a future?

Saudi Arabia has some of the largest reserves of oil in the world.

How much is left?

If oil is used at the current rate, and without the discovery of new oil fields, experts predict the world's supply will last until 2050. About two thirds of remaining known reserves are in the Middle East, the world's largest being Saudi Arabia's Ghawar oil field.

Alternative oil sources

As oil production slows and petroleum becomes more expensive to **extract**, oil reserves that were once thought to be too difficult and expensive to extract are now being explored. Two of these sources are oil shales and tar sands.

Oil shales and tar sands

Oil shales are rocks with an oil-like chemical trapped inside. Although expensive and environmentally harmful to access, shale oil can be a substitute for crude oil.

Petroleum can also be found as a semi-solid substance mixed with sand, known as oil sands or tar sands. This type of oil is also expensive and environmentally harmful to extract.

An oil sands development in northern Alberta, Canada.

Alternatives to oil

Oil does have a future in the short term. But in the long term, to depend less on oil, we need to invest in alternatives, such as **biofuels** and **fuel cells**, along with electric cars, buses, and boats. Iceland's fishing fleet, for example, has fuel-cell-powered electric engines for back-up power, and the country intends to make all its ships fuel-cell powered.

Solar panels on a ferry enable it to be powered by the sun.

Oil pros and cons

Pros

- Oil is still abundant for now.
- It is easy to use, store, and transport.
- It makes our modes of transportation go faster, and for longer periods.

Cons

- When burned it emits carbon dioxide, which is one cause of **climate change,** although it produces less carbon dioxide than coal does.
- It is non-renewable, so it will run out one day.
- It can be dangerous to people and a hazard to the environment.

Further information

BOOKS

Energy for Everyone? The Business of Energy by Nick Hunter, Franklin Watts, 2015

Burning Out: Energy from Fossil Fuels by Nancy Dickmann, Crabtree Publishing, 2016

Energy in Crisis by Catherine Chambers, Crabtree Publishing, 2010

Is There a Future for Fossil Fuels? by Ellen Rodger, Crabtree Publishing, 2010

WEBSITES

Go here for fun facts about crude oil:
www.funkidslive.com/events/crude-oil-energy-fact-file/

Explore renewable and non-renewable energy at:
www.eschooltoday.com/natural-resources/what-is-a-natural-resource.html

Learn about petroleum products at:
www.eia.gov/kids/energy.cfm?page=oil_home-basics

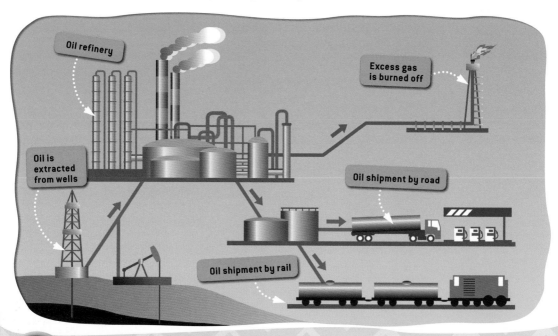

Oil refinery

Excess gas is burned off

Oil is extracted from wells

Oil shipment by road

Oil shipment by rail

Glossary

additive A substance added to something in small quantities to make it better

air pressure The force exerted by air

aqueduct A human-made channel that carries water

bacteria Tiny, single-celled living things that are found everywhere—some cause diseases

biofuel A fuel made from living things

bitumen A thick black substance used to surface roads, also known as asphalt or tar

blowout The uncontrolled release of crude oil from an oil well after pressure control systems have failed

brine Very salty water

climate change A process in which the environment changes. This can occur naturally, or it can be caused by human activity

derrick A framework or tower over an oil well which holds the drilling machinery

extract Remove

flammable Catches fire easily

fossil fuel A natural fuel, such as coal or natural gas, made from plants or animals that died millions of years ago

fuel cell A device that produces electricity directly from a chemical reaction

geologist A scientist who studies rocks and the history and structure of Earth

larvae Young animals that look very different from their parents, but will change later to look just like them

mass-produce Make large quantities of a product quickly and cheaply

natural gas Gas that occurs naturally under the ground

non-renewable Cannot be replaced; once used it is gone

petroleum A liquid mixture present in some rocks underground; can be extracted and refined to produce fuels, including gasoline and diesel

plankton Tiny plants or animals that float in oceans or lakes

pollute To make harmful for living things

porous Allows water or gas to pass through

prospector Someone who explores an area for oil or precious rocks and minerals, such as gold

reservoir A place where large amounts of a fluid collects

submersible Small submarine used for exploring under the sea

synthetic A human-made substance that copies a natural substance

tundra The vast treeless lands of the Arctic, where much of the soil is permanently frozen

valve A device to stop or slow the flow of gases or liquids in a pipe

wellhead The structure over an oil well

Index

A, B

asphalt 6–8, 21
barrels 15–19, 21
biofuel 5, 28
bitumen 6–8, 19, 21
blowouts 9, 12, 24

D, E

diesel 4, 18, 19–23
Drake, Edwin 9
extraction 12–13, 28

F

firestorm 25
Ford, Henry 9
fossil fuels 6
fuels 4–5, 14, 18–24, 26,
28–29

G, K

gas pump 4, 18, 20, 22, 24
gasoline 4, 14, 17–23
kerosene 19–21

O

oil refineries 16, 18–19, 25
oil rigs 4, 11, 24, 25
oil seeps 6–8, 10, 15
oil wells 9, 10, 12, 13, 24, 25

P

petroleum 4, 6, 8, 10, 12, 14,
15, 19, 20, 24, 26, 28
pipelines 16, 17, 22
prospectors 14

R, S

refineries 16, 18–19, 25
solar power 28, 29
sulfur 15, 18

T, W

tankers 17, 22, 24
transporting 9, 15–17, 29
wellheads 12, 13, 24
wind power 28